D1201882

U.S. Navy

BY LINDA BOZZO

amicus
high interest

Amicus High Interest is an imprint of Amicus
P.O. Box 1329, Mankato, MN 56002
www.amicuspublishing.us

Library of Congress Cataloging-in-Publication Data
Bozzo, Linda.
 U.S. Navy / Linda Bozzo.
    p. cm. -- (Serving in the military)
 Includes index.
 Audience: Grades K-3.
 Summary: "An introduction to what the US Navy is,
what recruits do, and jobs soldiers could learn. Includes
descriptions of missions to save a fishing crew from pirates
and to keep the oil shipping lane open"--Provided by
publisher.
 ISBN 978-1-60753-390-0 (library binding)
 1. United States. Navy--Juvenile literature. I. Title.
 VA58.4.B695 2014
 359.00973--dc23
                                    2012036374

Editor   Wendy Dieker
Series Designer   Kathleen Petelinsek
Page production   Red Line Editorial, Inc.

Photo Credits
Andrei Tsalko/Dreamstime, cover; Mass Communication
Specialist 3rd Class Tamara Vaughn/U.S. Navy, 5; U.S. Navy,
6; Mass Communication Specialist 3rd Class Paul Kelly/U.S.
Navy, 9; Mass Communication Specialist Seaman Apprentice
Ignacio D. Perez/U.S. Navy, 10; Mass Communication
Specialist 1st Class Andre N. McIntyre/U.S. Navy, 13; Mass
Communication Specialist 2nd Class Kilho Park/U.S. Navy, 14;
Mass Communication Specialist 3rd Class Trevor Welsh/U.S.
Navy, 17; Mass Communication Specialist Seaman Apprentice
Chris Salisbury/U.S. Navy, 19; Mass Communication Specialist
3rd Class Will Tyndall/U.S. Navy, 20; Mass Communication
Specialist 3rd Class John Philip Wagner Jr./U.S. Photo, 23;
Chief Mass Communication Specialist Jayme Pastoric/U.S.
Navy, 24; Mass Communication Specialist 1st Class Lynn
Friant/U.S. Navy, 27; Mass Communication Specialist 3rd
Class Darien G. Kenney/U.S. Navy, 28

Printed in the United States at Corporate Graphics in North
Mankato, Minnesota
5-2013 / 1150
10 9 8 7 6 5 4 3 2 1

Table of Contents

Pirates Attack!

It is January 2012 in the Arabian Sea. Pirates have taken over a fishing boat! Crew members are being forced to help the pirates. Their fishing boat is being used for more attacks. The U.S. Navy gets a call for help. The navy sailors must get a closer look.

A U.S. Navy radio operator gets
a call. She sends help right away.

The sailors fly in a helicopter. They hover above the boat. They see pirates! The fishers are in danger! More sailors are on a navy ship. They set out to save the fishers. They show the pirates their big guns. Soon, the pirates drop their weapons. They raise their hands in the air. They give up!

Pirates give up after seeing the *USS Kidd* coming with big guns.

A team of Navy SEALs gets on the fishing boat. They capture the pirates! The pirates are taken to another ship to be held prisoners. The fishing crew is saved! The fishers are given food and water. They head for home. Mission complete!

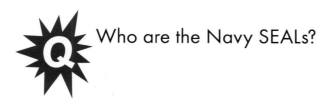 Who are the Navy SEALs?

A Navy SEAL climbs onto a boat with his gun drawn.

 SEALs are the best-trained sailors. They are named for where they work: Sea, Air, and Land.

Members of the U.S. Navy might become pilots after training camp.

Learning the Ropes

The U.S. Navy is always on call. They work to keep the seas safe, but you might see them on land or in the air too. What does it take to be a sailor? Plenty of training! The first step is to learn the job. Off to training camp.

New members of the navy are called **recruits**. "**Boot camp**" is where recruits train. They work hard for 7 to 9 weeks. They learn how to use **weapons**. New sailors learn how to stay alive in the water. They learn **seamanship**, or how to work on a ship. Men and women train hard to get fit.

 Why is training called "boot camp"?

Recruits even learn to march in formation.

 In the 1800s, sailors wore leggings called boots. New recruits trained in camps. People soon called these camps "boot camp."

A pilot tells his captain that he's ready to fly.

After boot camp, sailors go to "A" school to train for a navy job. Navy "A" schools are all over the country. There are hundreds of job choices. Most people train to work on ships. Some train to work on **submarines**. Others learn to fly planes.

After "A" school, a sailor may train to be an officer. That means more school. Officers lead other sailors and make important decisions.

Would you like to study the ocean? How about the weather? You could search for enemy submarines. You could work on an aircraft carrier. Maybe you have always dreamed of flying. You could fly a plane. Or a helicopter. Navy firefighters work on ships and submarines. All these jobs are navy jobs.

 What is an aircraft carrier?

A sailor plans a route for this aircraft carrier to follow.

 Aircraft carriers are like floating airports. Planes can take off and land in the middle of the ocean.

The Home Front

On the home front, a sailor's main job is to train to fight. But not everyone will go to battle. **Mechanics** keep equipment working. Office workers order things such as guns and food. Some sailors get ships ready for a mission. Tugboat crews are called to pull ships. But that is not all.

**Tug boats help pull a
submarine into port.**

Sailors help when disasters strike. They work as a team. Rescue swimmers drop from helicopters to save a fishing crew. After a hurricane, crews rescue people trapped in their homes. Some sailors are construction workers. They help rebuild after storms. Everyone has a job to do.

A rescue swimmer drops from a helicopter.

Stationed Overseas

Navy sailors work all over the world. Many live on aircraft carriers that are out to sea for months. Some live on overseas bases. Navy ships pull into base to get supplies. Sailors fuel planes and ships at bases. Weapons and bullets are stored at the base.

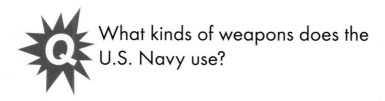

What kinds of weapons does the U.S. Navy use?

This aircraft carrier will be out to sea for months.

Submarines and destroyers use **torpedoes** and missiles underwater. Above the water, cruisers and destroyers fight with guns.

Out at sea, sailors can be close to wars. Enemies fire missiles. They might plant underwater **mines**. The navy's job is to fire back. They look for mines and disarm them. The navy keeps our country safe. On land, they may rebuild villages ruined by war. Navy police work to keep supply roads safe from attack.

The navy searches underwater for mines and explosives.

Wherever there is trouble, the U.S. Navy is called to help. Navy sailors keep other boats safe from pirate attacks. Many of the things we buy come from far away countries. Ships deliver these goods. Sailors work to keep these ships safe.

Sailors have their guns ready.
They watch for enemies.

Serving Our Country

In 2012, Iranian ships tried to keep the navy out of a waterway. Sailors feared Iran would block oil ships too. The navy ships did not leave. They made sure the United States got oil. The men and women of the U.S. Navy work hard to keep the oceans safe.

Navy heroes leave the *USS Carr*.

Glossary

boot camp Basic training for the navy.

mechanic A person who fixes machines like boats and planes.

mine An underwater weapon that explodes when a ship or submarine comes close.

recruit A person who has just joined the military.

seamanship The skill of working a ship.

submarine A navy vehicle that goes underwater.

torpedo A weapon that is used on a submarine.

weapon Something that a sailor uses to fight with, such as guns and bombs.

Read More

Goldish, Meish. *Navy: Civilian to Sailor.* New York, NY. Bearport Publishing, 2011.

Jackson, Kay. *Navy Ships in Action.* New York, NY. PowerKids Press, 2009.

Williams, Brian. *Sailors Under Fire.* Chicago, IL. Heinemann Library, 2012.

Websites

Brain Pop: Social Studies: Learn About the Armed Forces
http://www.brainpop.com/socialstudies/ usgovernmentandlaw/armedforces/preview.weml

Careers & Jobs: The U.S. Navy
http://www.navy.com/careers.html

Navy Sea Cadet Corps
http://www.seacadets.org/public/programs/nlcc/

Index

About the Author

Linda Bozzo is the author of more than 30 books for the school and library market. She would like to thank all of the men and women in the military for their outstanding service to our country. Visit Linda's website at www.lindabozzo.com.